N

[

FI

Hot and Cold

By Jack Challoner

Contents

RSVP
**RAINTREE
STECK-VAUGHN**
P U B L I S H E R S
The Steck-Vaughn Company

Austin, Texas

Published by Raintree Steck-Vaughn Publishers, an imprint of
Steck-Vaughn Company

Editors: Kim Merlino, Kathy DeVico
Project Manager: Lyda Guz
Electronic Production: Scott Melcer

Photo Credits: cover: The Stock Market: top Jose Fuste Raga;
Tony Stone Images: bottom;
Allsport: p. 4 Mike Powell;
FLPA: p. 22 David Hosking; pp. 24, 30 E. & D. Hosking;
Robert Harding Picture Library: pp. 18, 23, 25;
NHPA: p. 9 Peter Johnson; pp. 11, 15 E. A. Janes; p. 16 Anthony Bannister;
p. 27 Kevin Schafer; p. 28 Rod Planck; p. 29 David Woodfall;
p. 31 Stephen Dalton; Noel Peare: pp. 8, 19; Tony Stone Images: pp. 3, 26.

All other photographs by Claire Paxton.

Library of Congress Cataloging-in-Publication Data

Challoner, Jack.
Hot and cold / by Jack Challoner.
p.   cm. — (Start-up Science)
Includes index
ISBN 0-8172-4323-2
1. Heat — Experiments — Juvenile literature.   2. Cold — Experiments
— Juvenile literature.   3. Temperature — Experiments — Juvenile
literature.   [1. Heat — Experiments.   2. Cold — Experiments.
3. Temperature — Experiments.   4. Experiments.]   I. Title.
II. Series: Challoner, Jack. Start-up science.
QC271.4.C48   1997
536 — dc20
95-30013
CIP
AC

Printed in Spain
Bound in the United States
1 2 3 4 5 6 7 8 9 0 LB 99 98 97 96

Hot and Cold

This book will answer lots of questions that you may have about hot and cold things. But it will also make you think for yourself.

Each time you turn a page, you will find an activity that you can do yourself at home or at school. You may need help from an adult.

Is today a hot day, or do you feel cold? What makes you feel hot or cold?

What things do you know that are hot? What things do you know that are cold?

Hot Things

Many things around us feel hot. Hot things can be very dangerous. Warm things are not hot or cold, but somewhere in between.

Hot and sweaty

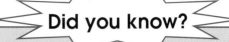
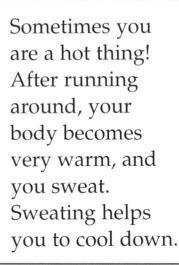

Sometimes you are a hot thing! After running around, your body becomes very warm, and you sweat. Sweating helps you to cool down.

Hot and smooth

Some people iron their clothes. The hot iron flattens out the creases when it is pressed on the clothes.

Now try this

If you have cold hands, you can warm them by rubbing them together.

Rub your hands together quickly. The harder you rub them, the warmer they will become.

Cold Things

On hot days, cold things such as ice pops or cold water can make us feel cool. But when it is cold outside, we need to keep warm.

Cooling down

Ice pops are made with frozen water, which is called **ice**. On a hot day, eating ice pops can help you to cool down.

Windy day

On some cold days, the wind blows and makes us feel even colder. This girl is dressed in thick clothes. They help protect her from the cold air.

Now try this

Some materials take heat away from your skin more quickly than others, which makes them feel cold.

You will need:
a clean handkerchief,
a metal spoon

1. Put the spoon and the handkerchief in the refrigerator for about half an hour.

2. Take both items out of the refrigerator, and hold them in your hands. Each is as cold as the other. But the metal spoon feels colder, because it takes heat away from your hands more quickly.

Melting and Freezing

You have probably seen water as a solid (ice) as well as a liquid. Liquids can freeze to become solids. Many solids can melt to become liquid.

Hot metal

Metals melt when they are really hot. When they cool, they become solid again. This metal is being made into a useful shape.

Melting ice

These icicles are made of ice. They have begun to melt and turn back into liquid water.

Chocolate is a solid, just like ice. It can melt to become liquid.

You will need:
a piece of chocolate

1. Hold the chocolate in your hand for a few minutes.

2. The chocolate will melt as it takes heat from your hand.

3. Make sure that you wash your hands afterward.

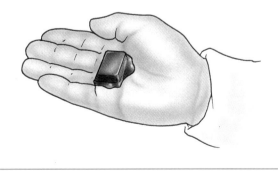

Hot or Cold?

People and most other animals can tell the difference between hot and cold. This can be very important. If animals or people become too hot or too cold, they may die.

Did you know?

Just beneath the surface of our skin, we have **nerves**. They allow us to feel whether things are hot or cold.

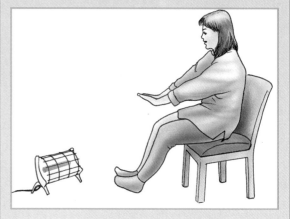

Not too hot

This woman is using her elbow to test the water in a baby's bathtub. Nerves in her skin tell her if the water is too hot or too cold.

Warm eggs

Before chicks can hatch, their eggs must be kept warm — but not too hot, and not too cold. This hen can feel when her eggs are just warm enough.

Warm water feels hot to a cold hand, and it feels cold to a hot hand.

You will need:
three bowls, ice cubes,
a sink with hot and cold water

1. Ask an adult to fill one bowl with ice-cold water, a second bowl with lukewarm water, and the last bowl with very warm (but not hot) water.

2. Put one hand in the cold water and one in the very warm water. Leave them there for a minute.

3. Now put both hands in the lukewarm water. How does each hand feel?

What Is Temperature?

The **temperature** of something is how hot or cold it is. **Thermometers** are used to measure temperature. The hotter something is, the higher its temperature is.

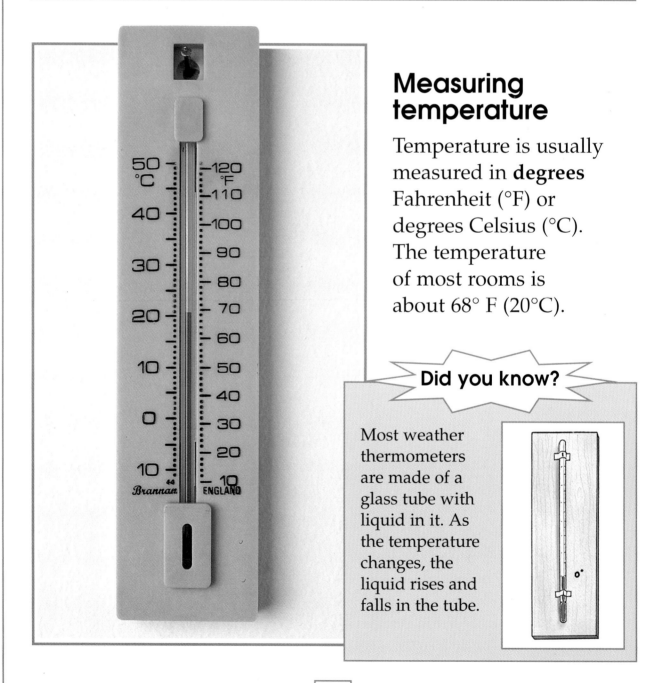

Measuring temperature

Temperature is usually measured in **degrees** Fahrenheit (°F) or degrees Celsius (°C). The temperature of most rooms is about 68° F (20°C).

Did you know?

Most weather thermometers are made of a glass tube with liquid in it. As the temperature changes, the liquid rises and falls in the tube.

Water temperature

There are many different types of thermometers. This one shows the temperature of the water in a fish tank. The water is about 66°F (19°C).

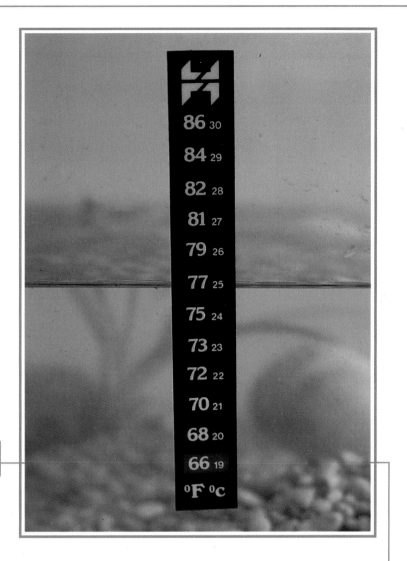

86	30
84	29
82	28
81	27
79	26
77	25
75	24
73	23
72	22
70	21
68	20
66	19
°F	°C

Now try this

Watch the temperature of water as it cools.

You will need:
a liquid crystal aquarium thermometer, ice cubes, warm and cold water, a clear glass or a plastic bowl, tape

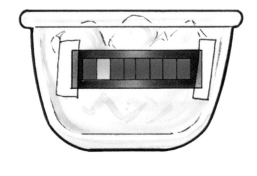

1. Tape the thermometer to the inside of the bowl.

2. Fill the bowl with warm water. Make a note of how warm the water feels and its temperature.

3. Ask an adult to add ice cubes to the water, and wait for about ten minutes. Feel the water, and read the temperature again.

BE SAFE!

Never touch something to find out how hot or cold it is.

Keeping Warm

On a cold day, your body loses heat easily, and you feel cold. Wrapping yourself in thick clothing is called **insulation**. People insulate their houses, too.

Did you know?

The walrus has a thick layer of fat. The fat insulates it from the cold water in which it swims.

Wrapped up

Wool is a good insulator because it contains a lot of air spaces. That is why it is used to make clothes worn in the cold weather.

Warm coats

These sheep have thick coats of wool. They help the sheep to keep warm in cold weather.

Now try this

You can see for yourself why wool is a good insulator.

You will need:
a wool glove, a bowl of water

1. Hold the glove above the water, and squeeze it.

2. Now hold the glove under the water, and squeeze it. You should see bubbles of air coming from the glove under the water.

Cooling Down

If you are really hot, you need something cold to take the heat away. You can use cold water or a cool drink to cool yourself down.

Cold shower

A fan cools you down as it blows the air past your body. The faster the air moves, the cooler you feel.

This elephant is cooling off by spraying itself with water. The water takes heat away from its body.

Ice cool

When the weather is really hot, you can cool down with a cold drink. Ice cubes take heat from the drink, making it even colder.

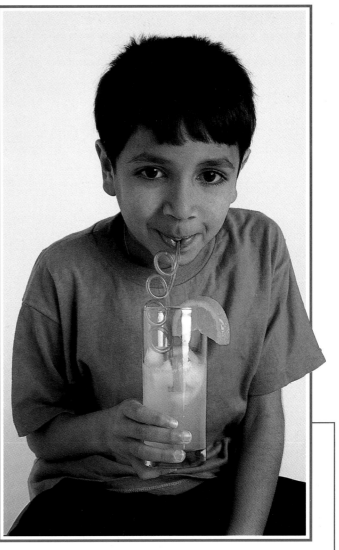

Now try this

When water leaves a warm wet cloth to become part of the air, it takes heat with it.

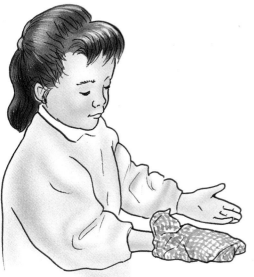

You will need:
a cloth, warm water

1. Ask an adult to soak the cloth in the warm water.

2. Wrap the cloth around one hand. Leave the other hand dry.

3. Now move both hands around in the air. Which one feels colder?

Fire and Heat

Three things are needed for a fire to start: something that will burn, called **fuel**, heat, and a gas, called oxygen, in the air.

Fighting fires

Firefighters spray cold water on fires. Water takes heat from the fire and keeps air from getting to it.

Forest fire

A fire in a forest can spread quickly, as the heat sets more and more dry wood on fire.

Now try this

The fuel for a candle is the wax, which is used up as it burns.

You will need:

a tall candle, a candleholder, paper, a pen or pencil

1. Lay the candle on a piece of paper, and draw around it.

2. Ask an adult to light the candle, and leave it burning somewhere safe.

3. After an hour, blow out the candle. When it has cooled, draw around it again, and compare the two drawings.

BE SAFE!
Never play with fire.

Food and Heat

Some of the food we eat is hot, and some is cold. Much of the cold food that we eat, such as bread, was hot when it was cooked. Cooking food changes it.

Did you know?

The food you eat produces heat, which helps to keep your body warm.

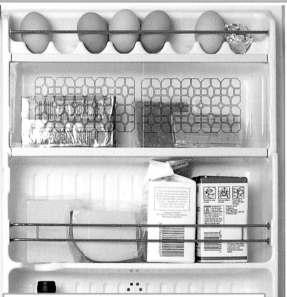

Keeping food fresh

At room temperature, foods go bad in a few days. A refrigerator keeps food cold, which keeps it fresh longer.

Changing food

Cake batter is put into a hot oven. In the oven, it will change to become a cake, like the one on the lower shelf. What other foods change when they are heated?

Now try this

How does heat get to the food inside a cooking pot?

You will need:
a metal cooking pot,
a plastic or wooden bowl,
a jug of warm water

1. Use both hands to hold the metal pot over a sink.

2. Ask an adult to pour some warm tap water into the pot. What do you feel?

3. Now do the same with the bowl. Do your hands feel warm more quickly or more slowly?

Heat from the Sun

Hot things, such as the sun, give out a kind of energy called **radiation**.

Some of the sun's radiation reaches the Earth and causes it to heat up.

In the sunshine

This lizard lives in the desert. It rests in the sunlight during the day to warm its body.

Did you know?

On a sunny day, you feel cooler if you wear white clothes than if you wear black clothes. Why do you think this is?

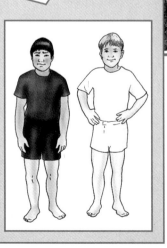

Hot water

The panels on the roof of this house have water flowing through them. The sun's radiation heats up the water, which can be used inside the house.

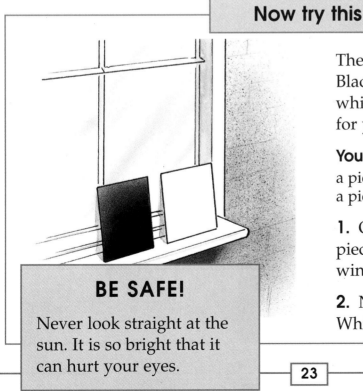

The sun's radiation heats things. Black things heat up more than white things. You can test this for yourself.

You will need:
a piece of black cardboard,
a piece of white cardboard

1. On a warm day, leave both pieces of cardboard out on a sunny windowsill for about an hour.

2. Now feel each one of them. Which piece feels warmer?

BE SAFE!

Never look straight at the sun. It is so bright that it can hurt your eyes.

Hot Places

The hottest places on the Earth are places the sun heats up the most. There are also hot places where heat comes from beneath the ground.

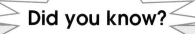

Did you know?

Deep under the ground, it is very hot. In some places, such as inside volcanoes, heat comes to the surface.

Hot geyser

Water deep under the ground can get very hot. Sometimes the hot water and steam shoot out from the surface. This is called a **geyser**.

Desert heat

Much of the time there are no clouds in the sky above deserts. This means that most deserts get very hot during the day.

Now try this

On a cold day, see how much warmer it is inside your home than it is outdoors.

You will need:
an aquarium thermometer

1. Find somewhere safe indoors to leave the thermometer. After a few minutes, read the temperature.

2. Now leave the thermometer somewhere safe outside. Make sure it is in the shade. What is the temperature outside?

Cold Places

At the top and bottom of the world are the North and South poles. There are always ice and snow here. It is also cold at the tops of mountains.

High places

The higher up a mountain you go, the colder it is. This is Mount Everest, in Nepal.

At 29,000 feet (8,848 m) high, it is the highest mountain in the world.

Keeping warm

These penguins live in the Antarctic, around the South Pole. It is the coldest part of the world. They are standing together, trying to keep warm.

Now try this

See what happens to water when it is very cold.

You will need:
some Popsicle® sticks, an ice cube tray, a jug, lemonade mix, water, a freezer

1. Mix some lemonade in the jug, and fill the ice cube tray with it. Cover the tray with a piece of plastic wrap. Put a Popsicle® stick in each section.

2. Place the tray in the freezer, and leave it there for a day.

The lemonade will have frozen onto the sticks.

Snow and Ice

When the temperature of liquid water falls below 32°F (0°C), it freezes to become ice. **Snow** is made of millions of beautiful pieces of ice.

Snowfall

Many clouds are made of tiny bits of ice. On a warm day, the ice melts on its way to the ground, and it falls as rain. But on a cold day, it falls as snow.

Frozen pond

The water under the ice in this pond is still liquid, so the fish in the pond will not die.

Now try this

When water freezes, it takes up more space. You can test this yourself.

You will need:
a plastic bottle (not a glass one), a freezer

1. Fill the plastic bottle with water right to the top. Ask an adult to stand it carefully in the freezer. Do not put the lid on the bottle.

2. The next day, look at the bottle. The water will have changed to ice, and the ice will be sticking out of the top of the bottle.

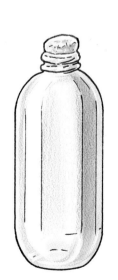

How Animals Survive

Some parts of the world are very cold, while other places are hot. Animals have many different ways of surviving weather that is too hot or too cold.

Big ears

This desert fox has very big ears, which help it to lose heat to the air. If it did not lose enough heat, the fox could die.

Long rest

Many animals, like this mouse, **hibernate** for the coldest months of the year.

Now try this

Some animals hibernate in feathers or straw. Find out how this insulation keeps them warm.

You will need:
two plastic jars (one with a lid), warm water, a wool sweater

1. Fill the jars with warm water.

2. Put the lid on one jar, and wrap it in the sweater. Do not put a lid on, or wrap up, the other jar.

3. Leave the jars in a cool place for an hour. Then feel the water in each jar. Which one is warmer?

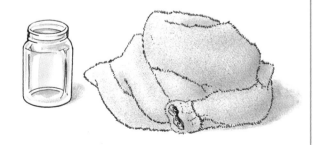

Glossary

degrees Units used to measure temperature

fuel A substance that provides heat or energy when it is burned

geyser A hot water spring

hibernate To spend the winter sleeping

ice Water that has frozen to become a solid

insulation A material used to prevent heat, light, or sound from escaping

nerves Parts of the body that send messages to the brain

radiation A type of light that spreads in all directions and heats things

snow Partly frozen water

temperature A measurement of heat or cold

thermometers Devices used to measure temperature

Index